CPSIA information can be obtained
at www.ICGtesting.com
Printed in the USA
LVHW100319211020
669278LV00001B/70

9 783347 159495